Copyright © 2011 XAMonline, Inc.
All rights reserved. No part of the material protected by this copyright notice may be reproduced or utilized in any form or by any means, electronic or mechanical, including photocopying, recording or by any information storage and retrievable system, without written permission from the copyright holder.

To obtain permission(s) to use the material from this work for any purpose including workshops or seminars, please submit a written request to:

XAMonline, Inc.
25 First Street, Suite 106
Cambridge, MA 02141
Toll Free: 1-800-509-4128
Email: info@xamonline.com
Web: www.xamonline.com
Fax: 1-617-583-5552

Library of Congress Cataloging-in-Publication Data

Wynne, Sharon A.
    PRAXIS ParaPro Assessment 0755 Practice Test 2: Teacher Certification /
    Sharon A. Wynne. -1st ed.
    ISBN: 978-1-60787-128-6
    1. PRAXIS ParaPro Assessment 0755 Practice Test 2   2. Study Guides
    3. PRAXIS   4. Teachers' Certification & Licensure   5. Careers

Disclaimer:
The opinions expressed in this publication are the sole works of XAMonline and were created independently from the National Education Association, Educational Testing Service, or any State Department of Education, National Evaluation Systems or other testing affiliates.

Between the time of publication and printing, state specific standards as well as testing formats and website information may change that is not included in part or in whole within this product. Sample test questions are developed by XAMonline and reflect similar content as on real tests; however, they are not former tests. XAMonline assembles content that aligns with state standards but makes no claims nor guarantees teacher candidates a passing score. Numerical scores are determined by testing companies such as NES or ETS and then are compared with individual state standards. A passing score varies from state to state.

Printed in the United States of America   œ-1
PRAXIS ParaPro Assessment 0755 Practice Test 2
ISBN: 978-1-60787-128-6

Praxis ParaPro Assessment (0755)
Post-Test Sample Questions

READING

Directions: Read the following passage and answer questions 1-6.

What is your favorite color? Is it blue? One of the most popular colors is blue. Blue is associated with things that are cold but, it also has a calming soothing effect on people. People associate their bedrooms with a place where they want to be calm and relaxed. Many people paint their bedrooms blue for this reason. However, even though blue is known for creating a tranquil and peaceful environment, when blue is associated with food we often think that it is spoiled or rotten. As a matter of fact, in a study conducted by scientists, food that was dyed blue and then served to people caused the participants to lose their appetites.

    The American Flag was not made haphazardly. It has a large patch of blue where 50 stars reside. Blue was purposefully used to symbolize justice, perseverance, and vigilance. Consequently, there are six white stripes and seven red stripes used in the flag. White was purposely used to symbolize purity and innocence, and red was used to represent valor and hardiness; all characteristics of the United States.

1. **What is the main idea of the passage?**
   (Average) (Skill 1.1)

   A. Many people's favorite color is blue

   B. Colors are symbolic of feelings and traits

   C. People do not like to eat blue food

   D. The American flag was purposefully made

2. **Why did the author write this passage?**
   (Rigorous) (Skill 1.1)

   A. To educate

   B. To narrate

   C. To entertain

   D. To describe

3. Which detail supports the idea that the American Flag's colors were chosen with a purpose in mind?
(Rigorous) (Skill 1.2)

   A. There are 50 stars on the American Flag

   B. There are 13 red and white stripes on the American Flag

   C. The color blue represents justice, perseverance, and vigilance

   D. The United States is a brave, pure and innocent country

4. What type of organizational pattern is used in the passage?
(Rigorous) (Skill 1.3)

   A. Compare and contrast

   B. Classification

   C. Cause and effect

   D. Sequence of events

5. During talks and speeches political parties often like to *vilify*, say slandering remarks, about the opposing party.

   What does the word *vilify* in the sentence above mean?
(Easy) (Skill 1.4)

   A. To speak to

   B. To campaign

   C. Put down

   D. Encourage

6. What type of context clue is presented in the sentence above?
(Rigorous) (Skill 1.4)

   A. Synonym

   B. Antonym

   C. Definition

   D. Example

Directions: Read the following passage and answer questions 7-10.

You might think that that an easy-going, laid back, unstructured summer is good for children. But chances are, due to our lack of routine and structure, children's sleep habits often suffer. Don't let your summer turn into the "dog days of summer" like mine have before. Be sure that your children get enough sleep even during the unstructured months of June, July, and August.

    Of course not all children are the same and do not require the same amount of sleep. I was surprised to learn that a 5-year old still needs about 11 hours of sleep a night. That means that if Rachel goes to bed at 8:00 then she should sleep until about 7:00 the next morning. Or if she goes to bed at 9:30 she should sleep until about 8:30 the next morning. If this isn't the case, there are a couple of things that can be done to help a child catch up. Options include, taking a nap during the day, put children to bed at an early hour, never wake a sleeping child, and keep daily activities limited. Remember, children who are well rested have better temperaments and are much more enjoyable to be around.

7. **What is MOST LIKELY true based on the above passage?**
   (Rigorous) (Skill 1.5)

   A. The author is a parent

   B. The author is a pediatrician

   C. The author is a teacher

   D. The author has twins

8. **What will most likely happen if a young child does not get enough sleep?**
   (Easy) (Skill 1.5)

   A. They won't be able to sleep well at night.

   B. They will be fine and make it through the day.

   C. They will get sick more easily.

   D. They will misbehave and act irrational.

9. **The author was surprised to learn that a 5-year-old still needs about 11 hours of sleep. Does this sentence contain a fact or an opinion?**
   (Average) (Skill 1.6)

   A. Fact

   B. Opinion

10. The author says, "that children who are well rested have better temperaments and are much more enjoyable to be around." Is this statement a fact or an opinion?
    (Easy) (Skill 1.6)

    A. Fact

    B. Opinion

Winter Olympic Medal Count by Country

		Gold	Silver	Bronze	Total
1.	United States	7	9	10	26
2.	Germany	7	9	7	23
3.	Norway	6	5	6	17

12. Which country earned the most medals in the 2010 Winter Olympic games?
    (Easy) (Skill 1.7)

    A. United States

    B. Germany

    C. Norway

    D. Switzerland

AGE	TOTAL HOURS OF SLEEP	DAY TIME(NAPS) HOURS
1 week	16.5	8
1 month	15.5	6
3 months	15	5
6 months	14.25	3-4
9 months	14	3
12 months	13.75	2-3
18 months	13.5	2
2 years	13	1-2
3 years	12	1
4 years	11.5	
5 years	11	
6 years	10.75	
7 years	10.5	
8 years	10.25	
9 years	10	
10 years	9.75	
11 years	9.5	
12 years	9.25	
13 years	9.25	
14 years	9	
15 years	8.75	
16 years	8.5	
17 years	8.25	
18 years	8.25	

13. Which countries have the same number of gold medals?
    (Easy) (Skill 1.7)

    A. United States and Norway

    B. Norway and Germany

    C. United States and Germany

    D. None

11. Using the chart above, how many hours of sleep a day should a 3 year old have?
    (Easy) (Skill 1.7)

    A. 11.5 hours

    B. 13 hours

    C. 12 hours

    D. 12.5 hours

14. **Which of the following are considered basic phonological awareness tasks?**
    (Average) (Skill 2.1)

    A. The ability to hear rhymes and alliteration

    B. The ability to blend sounds and split syllables

    C. The ability to locate words within words

    D. All of the above

15. **Which root means "land"?**
    (Average) (Skill 2.2)

    A. -bio-

    B. -terr-

    C. -audi-

    D. -omni-

16. **When is the best time for a teacher to introduce vocabulary words to readers?**
    (Rigorous) (Skill 2.2)

    A. Before reading

    B. During reading

    C. After reading

    D. All of the above.

17. **Context clues refer to:**
    (Average) (Skill 2.3)

    A. Defining new words using the dictionary

    B. Choosing the meaning of words pre-selected choices

    C. Creating a list of vocabulary from the text

    D. Defining unknown words based on the surrounding text

18. **When students understand how sentences are built and the words needed for the sentences to "sound" right, they have developed a sense of:**
    (Average) (Skill 2.3)

    A. Morphology

    B. Syntax

    C. Semantics

    D. Fluency

19. A teacher has letter tiles and she distributes some to students so they can participate in a making and breaking words activity. This activity is especially helpful in supporting which phase of reading?
    (Average) (Skill 2.3)

    A. Orthographic phase

    B. Analyzing phase

    C. Logographic phase

    D. Emergent reader phase

20. What pattern in spelling does C-V-C represent?
    (Average) (Skill 2.3)

    A. Consonant vowel combination

    B. Compare verbs critically

    C. Consonant vowel consonant

    D. Continent vowel component

21. Which homograph will fit in the blanks?
    (Rigorous) (Skill 2.4)

    Please get to the _____.
    The pencil _____ is sharp.

    A. summit

    B. tip

    C. point

    D. top

22. When a teacher refers to one-to-one corresponding in reading what is she referring to?
    (Rigorous) (Skill 2.5)

    A. One-to-one reading conferences with students

    B. One-to-one letter sound relationship in spelling

    C. One-to-one reading/pointing of a word to what is on the page

    D. One-to-one matching of students to an appropriate text

23. What is the purpose of before reading activities?
    (Rigorous) (Skill 2.6)

    A. To check if a text is appropriate for a student

    B. To activate background knowledge of readers

    C. To give them a task to complete during reading

    D. To give students a list of vocabulary words to learn

24. **What does "Story Mapping" have children do?**
    (Rigorous) (Skill 2.7)

    A. The students retell the story details

    B. Identify the characters, setting, problem and solution

    C. Identify the main idea and supporting details

    D. Draw a map to show what the characters did

25. **What are the two basic types of questions?**
    (Rigorous) (Skill 2.7)

    A Easy and hard questions

    B Verbal and written questions

    C In the book and in the reader's head

    D. Teacher made and student made

26. **What is the definition of synthesis?**
    (Average) (Skill 2.8)

    A. Pulling different ideas into one

    B. Putting a lot of different opinions together

    C. Taking a whole and pulling it apart

    D. Oral reading using various voices

27. **Book reviews are a good source for teaching students about valid and invalid opinions.**
    (Average) (Skill 2.8)

    A. True

    B. False

28. **In what book would students locate alternative synonyms for words?**
    (Average) (Skill 2.9)

    A. Almanac

    B. Dictionary

    C. Thesaurus

    D. Encyclopedia

29. **What words should students look for to help direct the next step in a written direction?** *(Average) (Skill 2.10)*

   A. Next

   B. Then

   C. Finally

   D. All of the above

30. **What are students expected to do when a directive reads, "Support your answer with evidence from the story"?** *(Rigorous) (Skill 2.10)*

   A. Write a one-word response

   B. Recall from memory what they read

   C. Find a few examples in the story and include them in the answer

   D. Name the characters, setting, problem, and solution that are present in the story

MATH

1. Evaluate:

    $$\frac{1}{3} - \frac{1}{2} + \frac{1}{6}$$

    (Average) (Skill 3.1)

    A. 5/6

    B. 2/3

    C. 0

    D. 1

2. Express in symbols: "x is greater than seven and less than or equal to fifteen".
    (Easy) (Skill 3.3)

    A. $7 < x \leq 15$

    B. $7 > x \geq 15$

    C. $15 \leq x < 7$

    D. $7 < x = 15$

3. "Twice the product of two positive numbers is equal to the square of their sums." This statement is:
    (Average) (Skill 3.4)

    A. Always true

    B. Sometimes true

    C. Never true

    D. Meaningless

4. The digit 4 in the number 302.41 is in the
    (Easy) (Skill 3.5)

    A. Tenths place

    B. Ones place

    C. Hundredths place

    D. Hundreds place

5. A carton of milk priced at $6.00 is 30% off. Another carton priced at $5.80 is 20% off. Which one is the better buy?
    (Rigorous) (Skill 3.6)

    A. The $5.80 carton

    B. The $6.00 carton

    C. Both are equal

    D. There is not enough information

6. Simplify:

    $$\frac{2^{-4} \times 4^2 \times 8}{4^{-2}}$$

    (Average) (Skill 3.7)

    A. 2^7

    B. 32

    C. $\frac{1}{8}$

    D. 2

7. Simplify:

$$\frac{(-2)^3 + 4^2}{3 - 5^2 + 3 \bullet 6}$$

(Rigorous) (Skill 3.8)

A. 1/2

B. -2

C. -3.5

D. 24

8. Marvin bought a bag of candy. He gave half of the pieces to his friend Mike and one-third of the pieces to his sister Lisa. He ate half of the remaining pieces and had 15 left. How many pieces of candy were in the bag in the beginning?
(Rigorous) (Skill 3.10)

A. 120

B. 90

C. 30

D. 180

9. Solve for x:

7 + 3x – 6 = 3x + 5 – x

(Average) (Skill 3.11)

A. 2.5

B. 4

C. 4.5

10. 27

10. What is the next term in the sequence:

$$\frac{2}{7}, \frac{13}{21}, \frac{20}{21}, \frac{9}{7}, \ldots$$

(Rigorous) (Skill 3.12)

A. $\frac{29}{21}$

B. $\frac{17}{21}$

C. $\frac{11}{7}$

D. $\frac{34}{21}$

11. About how many seconds is a typical human lifespan? (Assume that the average person lives 75 years). *(Average) (Skill 4.2)*

    A. 2.5 billion

    B. 2.5 million

    C. 2.5 trillion

    D. 250 million

12. Which of the following shapes is a rhombus?

    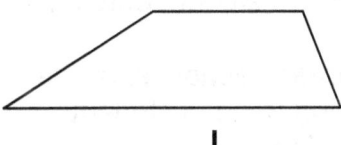

    I

    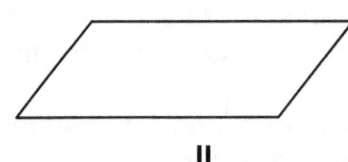

    II

    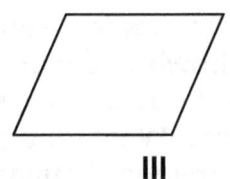

    III

    (Easy) (Skill 4.3)

    A. I

    B. II

    C. III

    D. None of the above

13. A solid object is shaped like a cone with the top cut off such that the top surface has a radius r_1 and the bottom surface has a radius r_2. If the height of the original cone is h and the height of the part cut off from the top is x, what the volume of the object?

    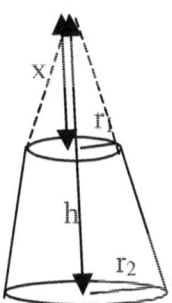

    (Rigorous) (Skill 4.4)

    A. $\frac{1}{3}\pi r_1^2 h - \frac{1}{3}\pi r_2^2 x$

    B. $\frac{1}{3}\pi r_2^2 h + \frac{1}{3}\pi r_1^2 x$

    C. $\frac{1}{3}\pi r_1^2 h + \frac{1}{3}\pi r_2^2 x$

    D. $\frac{1}{3}\pi r_2^2 h - \frac{1}{3}\pi r_1^2 x$

14. The slope of the line joining the two points shown on the coordinate plane below is (Rigorous) (Skill 4.5)

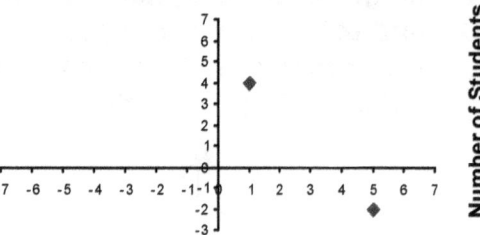

A. 3/2

B. -3/2

C. 2/3

D. -2/3

15. The stem and leaf plot below shows the heights of several children in a class in feet. What is the median height?

3	6 9
4	1 2 3 4 4 9
5	1 3 5

(Average) (Skill 5.1)

A. 4 ft

B. 4.9 ft

C. 4.4 ft

D. 5.1 ft

16. Which of the following statements is not true about the graph shown below? (Average) (Skill 5.2)

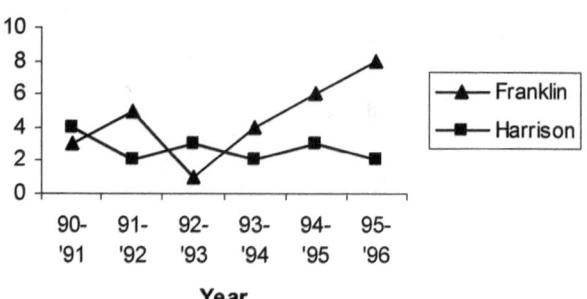

A. Franklin school shows a rising trend in student enrollment

B. Harrison school shows a falling trend in student enrollment

C. Both schools show similar trends in student enrollment

D. Neither school has had more than 900 students

17. You wish to create a visual display showing test score trends over several decades for a school. What kind of chart would be the most suitable? (Average) (Skill 5.3)

A. Circle graph

B. Bar graph

C. Histogram

D. Line graph

18. Which of these statements about the following data set is correct?

    2, 5, 12, 6, 3, 9, 5, 12, 20, 2, 3, 5, 21, 12

    (Rigorous) (Skill 5.4)

    A. There are 2 modes, the median is 8.5 and the range is 10

    B. There are 2 modes, the median is 5.5 and the range is 19

    C. There are 4 modes, the median is 5.5 and the range is 19

    D. There are 2 modes, the median is 5.5 and the range is 10

19. A student does the fraction addition $\frac{3}{5}+\frac{4}{15}+\frac{3}{4}$ and gets the answer 5/12. The most likely explanation for this mistake is:
    (Average) (Competency 6)

    A. The student added all the numerators together and all the denominators together

    B. The student subtracted the last fraction instead of adding

    C. The student multiplied the fractions

    D. None of the above

20. A student argues that the tenths place should be the second place to the right of the decimal point since the tens place is the second place to the left of the decimal point. How can you best explain why that is not the case?
    (Rigorous) (Competency 6)

    A. The decimal point stands for the missing place

    B. There is no "oneths" place since that would be the same as the ones place

    C. Each place, with or without the decimal point is a tenth of the place to its left

    D. There is no "zeroth" place

21. You are teaching a group of students how to solve percentage problems. Which of the following concepts would be most helpful to them?
    (Average) (Competency 6)

    A. To convert a fraction to percent, multiply by 100

    B. "percent" means "out of 100" and "of" implies multiplication

    C. A percentage problem is essentially a proportion problem with the percentage being the proportion out of 100

    D. To find a given percent of a particular number, divide the number by 100 and multiply by the number given

22. A student performs the computation

    $$\left(2^3\right)^5 = 2^8$$

    since exponents are supposed to be added.
    How would you explain the error?
    (Easy) (Competency 6)

    A. Say that if a second exponent is outside the parentheses, the two exponents must be multiplied

    B. Note that the following rule must be followed: $\left(a^m\right)^n = a^{mn}$

    C. Show that $\left(2^3\right)^5 = 8^5$

    D. Show that
    $\left(2^3\right)^5 = 2^3 \times 2^3 \times 2^3 \times 2^3 \times 2^3 = 2^{3+3+3+3+3}$

23. A student uses the mnemonic "PEDMSA" to remember the order of operations. Is she right?
    (Easy) (Competency 6)

    A. Yes

    B. No

    C. It depends on the problem

    D. Switching D and M would be fine but not switching A and S

24. A paraprofessional is helping students learn how to set up and solve systems of equations through the following word problem: "Three apples and two oranges cost $1.40. Four apples and three oranges cost $2.00. How much does one apple and one orange cost?"

    Which of the following steps would you use:

    I. Use the guess and check method to estimate the answer.
    II. Identify and name the variables.
    III. Write equations showing the relationships between the variables.
    IV. Subtract the cost of three apples and two oranges from the cost of four apples and three oranges.
    V. Solve the equations using substitution or elimination.
    (Rigorous) (Competency 6)

    A. I, II, III, and V

    B. II, III, and V

    C. I and IV

    D. IV

25. A student is solving the equation

    $x + 3 = 2(x + 3)$

    He divides both sides by $x + 3$ and gets 1 = 2. What is his mistake?
    (Rigorous) (Competency 6)

    A. He did not make any mistakes

    B. He inadvertently divided by zero

    C. One can never divide by an algebraic expression

    D. He should have first set $x + 3 = y$

26. You are helping a student find the next term in a given number sequence. A good first step would be to:
    (Easy) (Competency 6)

    A. Check and see whether the sequence is arithmetic or geometric

    B. Take the difference of the first two terms and add it to the last term

    C. Take the ratio of the first two terms and multiply the last term by it

    D. Check to see whether alternate terms are related

27. A paraprofessional is giving real life examples in order to explain the relative magnitude of the length units millimeter, centimeter, and meter. Which of the following sets would be the best choice?
    (Average) (Competency 6)

    A. Items on sale at a store

    B. Animals of different sizes

    C. Objects in a classroom

    D. Toys of various sizes

28. Students in a class are asked to draw the parallelogram with the largest possible area with longer sides 4 cm in length and shorter sides 2 cm in length. Student A draws a parallelogram with an internal angle of 90 degrees. Student B, C, and D draw parallelograms with internal angles of 45 degrees, 120 degrees, and 60 degrees respectively. Which student has the correct answer?
    (Rigorous) (Competency 6)

    A. A

    B. B

    C. C

    D. D

29. A student is computing the area of a right triangle on a coordinate plane defined by the points A (-1, 0), B (0, 2) and C (6, -1). Which of the following is the simplest method?
    (Rigorous) (Competency 6)

    A. Draw a perpendicular BD from B to AC and find the coordinates of D using the Pythagorean theorem on triangles ABD and DBC; find the height BD of the triangle; area = ½ x AC x BD

    B. The coordinate axes cut the triangle into four shapes; find the area of each shape and add them up

    C. Identify the two perpendicular sides using slopes and find their lengths; if one of the sides is the base, the other is the height; area = ½ x base x height.

    D. Find the equation of the line BC; find the point D at which the line BC intersects the y axis; find the areas of the triangles BAD and CBD and add them

30. You are helping a student graph yearly rainfall data in inches for a century. A good choice of scale for the x and y axes would be
    (Average) (Competency 6)

    A. Years along the x-axis with major tick marks every decade and inches along the y-axis with major tick marks every 5 inches

    B. Years along the y-axis with major tick marks every decade and inches along the x-axis with major tick marks every 5 inches

    C. Years along the x-axis with major tick marks every year and inches along the y-axis with major tick marks every 5 inches

    D. Years along the x-axis with major tick marks every decade and inches along the y-axis with major tick marks every inch

WRITING

1. What type of writing includes headings, subheadings, and titles?
   (Average) (Skill 1.7)

   A. Persuasive

   B. Descriptive

   C. Narrative

   D. Informative

2. Which word needs to be corrected in the sentence below?
   (Rigorous) (Skill 1.8)

   The Biggilow family were concerned with the appearance of their home.

   A. family

   B. were

   C. appearance

   D. their

3. Which word will complete the sentence?
   (Average) (Skill 1.8)

   It will be ____ cold for us to camp outside this weekend.

   A. too

   B. to

   C. two

   D. tow

4. Which sentence is punctuated incorrectly?
   (Easy) (Skill 1.8)

   A. Tomorrow night we'll have pizza for dinner?

   B. Close the door please.

   C. Go away!

   D. What time does the movie begin?

5. Which punctuation mark is required, if any, in the sentence?
   (Easy) (Skill 1.8)

   Let's have some chocolate graham crackers and marshmallows for dessert

   A. !

   B. ?

   C. ,

   D. None

6. What type of sentence is the sentence below?
   (Skill 1.8, Rigorous)

   Millie and Max seemed tired and bored.

   A. Simple

   B. Compound

   C. Complex

   D. Compound/complex

7. How would a letter to the editor be written?
   (Rigorous) (Skill 1.10)

   A. Using formal language

   B. Using informal/slang language

   C. Using informal language with informal mechanics

   D. Using words from the dialect of its intended audience

8. How do you write the plural form of the word *tornado*?
   (Easy) (Skill 7.1)

   A. Tornados

   B. Tornadoes

   C. Tornadose

   D. Tornadoz

9. Which word best completes the sentence?
   (Easy) (Skill 7.1)

   There were two _____ swimming in the fish bowl.

   A. fishes

   B. fish

   C. fishies

   D. fish's

10. Which word will complete the sentence?
    (Average) (Skill 7.2)

    We are so happy that _____ joining us on our annual vacation to the mountains.

    A. they're

    B. their

    C. there

    D. them

11. Carrie pointed to a house on Pritchett Drive and said, "I used to live there".

    Was Carrie's statement said correctly?
    (Easy) (Skill 7.2)

    A. Yes

    B. No

12. Which word will complete the sentence?
    (Rigorous) (Skill 7.3)

    The _____ live in a rocky area at the zoo.

    A. monkeys

    B. monkey's

    C. monkies

    D. monkie's

13. Which sentence is correct?
    (Rigorous) (Skill 7.3)

    A. Kids running around on a beautiful spring day.

    B. Kids run around on a beautiful spring day.

    C. Kids run, around on a beautiful spring day.

    D. Kids running. Around on a beautiful spring day.

14. What type of sentence is the sentence below?
    (Average) (Skill 7.4)

    While swimming in the pool, the children had a great time together.

    A. Simple

    B. Compound

    C. Complex

    D. Compound/Complex

15. What must be done to make this sentence correct?
    (Rigorous) (Skill 7.4)

    Meanwhile in the living room.

    A. Place a comma after meanwhile

    B. Change the word *living room* to *livingroom*

    C. Delete the period and add an independent clause

    D. Choice A and C

16. Which sentence is a run-on sentence?
(Rigorous) (Skill 7.4)

    A. I would like to have a grilled chicken salad for lunch what would you like.

    B. For lunch I had grilled chicken a diet soda and a bag of chips.

    C. Before lunch I washed my hands then I bought a soda.

    D. As soon as I finished my lunch I returned to my office to finish my work.

17. Which change, if any, would make the underlined words correct?
(Easy) (Skill 7.5)

    Them put their feet in the water while they ***was*** sitting on the dock.

    A. They...was

    B. Them...were

    C. They...were

    D. No change necessary

18. Which change, if any, would make the underlined word correct?
(Rigorous) (Skill 7.5)

    I can't believe that you brang that topic up at the staff meeting yesterday.

    A. bring

    B. brought

    C. brung

    D. No change necessary

19. Which word will make the sentence correct?
(Easy) (Skill 7.5)

    In the _____ the housing market was booming and people's profit margins were a lot larger.

    A. 1990's

    B. 1990s

    C. nineteen-nineties

    D. 19-nineties

20. Which sentence is written correctly?
    (Easy) (Skill 7.5)

    A. I gathered all the garbage together and thowed it all away.

    B. I gathered all the garbage together and through it all away.

    C. I gathered all the garbage together and threw it all away.

    D. I gathered all the garbage together and thrown it all away.

21. Which word will correctly complete the sentence?
    (Average) (Skill 7.5)

    We waited in the _____ office for over an hour for our appointment.

    A. doctores

    B. doctors

    C. doctors'

    D. doctor

Directions: Choose the correctly spelled word to complete each sentence for questions 22–26

22. For spring vacation, our family decided to visit a _____ island.
    (Average) (Skill 7.6)

    A. tropickal

    B. tropical

23. The sign at the intersection told us to _____ with caution.
    (Average) (Skill 7.6)

    A. proceed

    B. preceed

24. Queen Elizabeth became _____ when she tripped and fell down the winding, circular staircase.
    (Average) (Skill 7.6)

    A. embarassed

    B. embarrassed

25. She serves as a _____ for human resources and corporate headquarters.
    (Average) (Skill 7.6)

    A. liaison

    B. liason

26. The bag says that this recipe will _____ 6-dozen cookies.
    (Average) (Skill 7.6)

    A. yield

    B. yeild

27. When a student is going to write a non-fiction essay, what is the best way to organize their ideas?
    (Rigorous) (Skill 8.1)

    A. Create an outline

    B. Create a web

    C. Free write ideas on a topic

    D. All of the above

28. What is the purpose of prewriting before students draft?
    (Average) (Skill 8.1)

    A. It helps organize their ideas

    B. If they prewrite, they don't need to draft

    C. It will make their draft longer

    D. A prewrite and a draft are the same thing

29. What makes the organizer, or prewrite, for a personal narrative unique?
    (Rigorous) (Skill 8.1)

    A. It includes characters, setting, problem, and a solution

    B. It includes a beginning, middle, and end

    C. It outlines how the piece will be organized; for example, a circle story

    D. It lists out the sequence of events with headings.

30. A student is trying to find synonyms for the word *nice*. What is the best reference source use?
    (Rigorous) (Skill 8.2)

    A. A dictionary

    B. An atlas

    C. An almanac

    D. A thesaurus

31. Look at the dictionary entry below.

    chocolate [chaw-kuh-lit]

    1. a preparation of the seeds of cacao, roasted, husked, and ground, often sweetened and flavored, as with vanilla.

    How many syllables does the word chocolate have according to the dictionary entry?
    (Rigorous) (Skill 8.2)

    A. 1

    B. 2

    C. 3

    D. 4

32. **What is a revising strategy that students can use to improve their drafts?**
    (Rigorous) (Skill 8.3)

    A. Try different types of beginnings

    B. Read the piece backwards to focus on the spelling of each word

    C. Make sure that each sentence begins with a capital letter

    D. Make sure that each sentence has end punctuation

33. **What is the purpose of a thesis statement?**
    (Average) (Skill 8.3)

    A. To keep the writer focused

    B. To state the main idea of a paper

    C. To give the writer something to research

    D. To act as a hook

34. **In a five-paragraph essay, what are the middle paragraphs called?**
    (Average) (Skill 8.3)

    A. Thesis statement

    B. The introduction

    C. The body

    D The conclusion

35. **What is the first sentence in every body paragraph called?**
    (Average) (Skill 8.3)

    A. The main idea

    B. The thesis statement

    C. Opinion support statement

    D. The question statement

36. **Why must students edit their papers before they publish them?**
(Average) (Skill 8.4)

   A. To find pictures to use before the piece is published

   B. Because papers must be done in a student's neatest handwriting

   C. To improve the craft of writing

   D. To improve spelling, punctuation, and grammar

37. **What is the best way to edit a paper if it has been handwritten?**
(Rigorous) (Skill 8.4)

   A. Scan it and spell check it

   B. Have the teacher review it

   C. Read it backwards and have a peer review it

   D. Have an adult review the paper and make corrections

38. **How do authors determine whether their piece should be formal or informal?**
(Average) (Skill 8.5)

   A. Whether they will be graded by the teacher

   B. If the writer is trying to entertain, inform, or persuade

   C. By the language that was used in the piece of writing

   D. Whether the writing is formal or informal

39. **What is a persuasive technique that simply states the same idea many times only using different words each time to convey the same idea?**
(Rigorous) (Skill 8.6)

   A. Fallacious reasoning

   B. Only-cause fallacy

   C. Circular reasoning

   D. A hasty generalization

40. *There are a few holidays that recognize saints. For example, Valentine's Day recognizes Saint Valentine. St. Patrick's Day recognizes St. Patrick.*

    What type of writing is demonstrated in the passage above?
    (Rigorous) (Skill 8.6)

    A. Descriptive

    B. Narrative

    C. Informative

    D. Persuasive

Praxis ParaPro Assessment (0755)
Post-Test Sample Questions with Rationales

READING

Directions: Read the following passage and answer questions 1-6.

What is your favorite color? Is it blue? One of the most popular colors is blue. Blue is associated with things that are cold but, it also has a calming soothing effect on people. People associate their bedrooms with a place where they want to be calm and relaxed. Many people paint their bedrooms blue for this reason. However, even though blue is known for creating a tranquil and peaceful environment, when blue is associated with food we often think that it is spoiled or rotten. As a matter of fact, in a study conducted by scientists, food that was dyed blue and then served to people caused the participants to lose their appetites.

    The American Flag was not made haphazardly. It has a large patch of blue where 50 stars reside. Blue was purposefully used to symbolize justice, perseverance, and vigilance. Consequently, there are six white stripes and seven red stripes used in the flag. White was purposely used to symbolize purity and innocence, and red was used to represent valor and hardiness; all characteristics of the United States.

1. What is the main idea of the passage?
   (Average) (Skill 1.1)

   A. Many people's favorite color is blue

   B. Colors are symbolic of feelings and traits

   C. People do not like to eat blue food

   D. The American flag was purposefully made

Answer: B. Colors are symbolic of feelings and traits
This is the only choice that covers the whole passage. The other choices are details of the main idea.

2. **Why did the author write this passage?**
   (Rigorous) (Skill 1.1)

   A. To educate

   B. To narrate

   C. To entertain

   D. To describe

Answer: A. To educate
To educate is the same as informing. The author wrote this passage to inform its readers.

3. **Which detail supports the idea that the American Flag's colors were chosen with a purpose in mind?**
   (Rigorous) (Skill 1.2)

   A. There are 50 stars on the American Flag

   B. There are 13 red and white stripes on the American Flag

   C. The color blue represents justice, perseverance, and vigilance

   D. The United States is a brave, pure and innocent country

Answer: C. The color blue represents justice, perseverance, and vigilance
Choice C supports the main idea of the last paragraph that the American Flag's colors were chosen with a purpose in mind.

4. **What type of organizational pattern is used in the passage?**
   (Rigorous) (Skill 1.3)

   A. Compare and contrast

   B. Classification

   C. Cause and effect

   D. Sequence of events

Answer: B. Classification
In classification organization, the topic sentence usually states the general category and the rest of the sentences show how various elements of the category have a common base.

5. **During talks and speeches political parties often like to *vilify*, say slandering remarks, about the opposing party.**

   What does the word *vilify* in the sentence above mean?
   (Easy) (Skill 1.4)

   A. To speak to

   B. To campaign

   C. Put down

   D. Encourage

Answer: C. Put down
Slander, in the phrase after the word *vilify*, means to put down.

6. **What type of context clue is presented in the sentence above?** *(Rigorous) (Skill 1.4)*

    A. Synonym

    B. Antonym

    C. Definition

    D. Example

Answer: C. Definition
The word *vilify* is defined within the commas after it is presented in the sentence.

Directions: Read the following passage and answer questions 7-10.

You might think that that an easy-going, laid back, unstructured summer is good for children. But chances are, due to our lack of routine and structure, children's sleep habits often suffer. Don't let your summer turn into the "dog days of summer" like mine have before. Be sure that your children get enough sleep even during the unstructured months of June, July, and August.

Of course not all children are the same and do not require the same amount of sleep. I was surprised to learn that a 5-year old still needs about 11 hours of sleep a night. That means that if Rachel goes to bed at 8:00 then she should sleep until about 7:00 the next morning. Or if she goes to bed at 9:30 she should sleep until about 8:30 the next morning. If this isn't the case, there are a couple of things that can be done to help a child catch up. Options include, taking a nap during the day, put children to bed at an early hour, never wake a sleeping child, and keep daily activities limited. Remember, children who are well rested have better temperaments and are much more enjoyable to be around.

7. **What is MOST LIKELY true based on the above passage?**
   (Rigorous) (Skill 1.5)

   A.   The author is a parent

   B.   The author is a pediatrician

   C   The author is a teacher

   D   The author has twins

Answer: A. The author is a parent
The author sounds like they have experience handling tired children over the summer. Choice B might be true, but it isn't the best answer because the author doesn't offer any clinical information.

8. What will most likely happen if a young child does not get enough sleep?
   (Easy) (Skill 1.5)

   A. They won't be able to sleep well at night

   B. They will be fine and make it through the day

   C. They will get sick more easily

   D. They will misbehave and act irrational

Answer: D. They will misbehave and act irrational
The author puts the saying "The dog days of summer" in quotes to indicate that children who do not get enough sleep will most likely act like wild dogs.

9. The author was surprised to learn that a 5-year-old still needs about 11 hours of sleep. Does this sentence contain a fact or an opinion?
   (Average) (Skill 1.6)

   A. Fact

   B. Opinion

Answer: A. Fact
A 5-year-old requires about 11 hours sleep is a fact because it is verifiable.

10. The author says, "that children who are well rested have better temperaments and are much more enjoyable to be around."

    Is this statement a fact or an opinion?
    (Easy) (Skill 1.6)

    A. Fact

    B. Opinion

Answer: B. Opinion
The statement is an opinion because it is not verifiable, and it is what the author thinks and may not be shared by other people.

AGE	TOTAL HOURS OF SLEEP	DAY TIME(NAPS) HOURS
1 week	16.5	8
1 month	15.5	6
3 months	15	5
6 months	14.25	3-4
9 months	14	3
12 months	13.75	2-3
18 months	13.5	2
2 years	13	1-2
3 years	12	1
4 years	11.5	
5 years	11	
6 years	10.75	
7 years	10.5	
8 years	10.25	
9 years	10	
10 years	9.75	
11 years	9.5	
12 years	9.25	
13 years	9.25	
14 years	9	
15 years	8.75	
16 years	8.5	
17 years	8.25	
18 years	8.25	

11. Using the chart above, how many hours of sleep a day should a 3 year old have?
(Easy) (Skill 1.7)

A. 11.5 hours

B. 13 hours

C. 12 hours

D. 12.5 hours

Answer: C. 12 hours
The chart is broken into three columns; age, total hours of sleep, and daytime hours. 12 hours is the total hours of sleep for a 3 year old.

Winter Olympic Medal Count by Country

		Gold	Silver	Bronze	Total
1.	United States	7	9	10	26
2.	Germany	7	9	7	23
3.	Norway	6	5	6	17

12. Which country earned the most medals in the 2010 Winter Olympic games?
(Easy) (Skill 1.7)

    A. United States

    B. Germany

    C. Norway

    D. Switzerland

Answer: A. United States
The United States won the most medals; they won 26 medals.

13. Which countries have the same number of gold medals?
(Easy) (Skill 1.7)

    A. United States and Norway

    B. Norway and Germany

    C. United States and Germany

    D. None

Answer: C. United States and Germany
The United States and Germany both have 7 gold medals so far.

14. **Which of the following are considered basic phonological awareness tasks?**
    (Average) (Skill 2.1)

    A. The ability to hear rhymes and alliteration

    B. The ability to blend sounds and split syllables

    C. The ability to locate words within words

    D. All of the above

Answer: D. All of the above
All of the choices are considered to be basic phonological awareness tasks according to theorist Marilyn Jager who researches early reading.

15. **Which root means "land"?**
    (Average) (Skill 2.2)

    A. -bio-

    B. -terr-

    C. -audi-

    D. -omni-

Answer: B. -terr-
The answer -terr- means land, as in *all terrain vehicle*.

16. **When is the best time for a teacher to introduce vocabulary words to readers?**
    (Rigorous) (Skill 2.2)

    A. Before reading

    B. During reading

    C. After reading

    D. All of the above

Answer: D. All of the above
Before reading is not the only time that teachers can introduce vocabulary. Teachers can assign certain words for students to hunt for during reading, and can give them focus vocabulary words to examine after reading.

17. **Context clues refer to:**
    (Average) (Skill 2.3)

    A.   Defining new words using the dictionary

    B.   Choosing the meaning of words pre-selected choices

    C.   Creating a list of vocabulary from the text

    D.   Defining unknown words based on the surrounding text

Answer: D. Defining unknown words based on the surrounding text
Context clues are clues given within the text that allow readers to determine the meaning of unknown words. Good readers use this strategy rather than consulting a dictionary while in the middle of reading.

18. **When students understand how sentences are built and the words needed for the sentences to "sound" right, they have developed a sense of:**
    (Average) (Skill 2.3)

    A.   Morphology

    B.   Syntax

    C.   Semantics

    D.   Fluency

Answer: B. Syntax
Syntax refers to the rules or patterned relationships that correctly create phrases and sentences from words. When readers develop an understanding of syntax, they begin to understand the structure of how sentences are built.

19. A teacher has letter tiles and she distributes some to students so they can participate in a making and breaking words activity. This activity is especially helpful in supporting which phase of reading?
    (Average) (Skill 2.3)

    A. Orthographic phase

    B. Analyzing phase

    C. Logographic phase

    D. Emergent reader phase

Answer A: Orthographic phase
During the orthographic phase, students are able to use what they know about spelling patterns and letter relationships to help them with what they don't know.

20. What pattern in spelling does C-V-C represent?
    (Average) (Skill 2.3)

    A. Consonant vowel combination

    B. Compare verbs critically

    C. Consonant vowel consonant

    D. Continent vowel component

Answer: C. Consonant vowel consonant
Consonants are all letters that are NOT vowels. When talking about spelling patterns, C stands for consonant and V stands for vowel.

21. **Which homograph will fit in the blanks?**
    (Rigorous) (Skill 2.4)

    Please get to the _____.
    The pencil _____ is sharp.

    A. summit

    B. tip

    C. point

    D. top

Answer: C. point
Although other words may work in both sentences, point is the only homophone.

22. **When a teacher refers to one-to-one corresponding in reading what is she referring to?**
    (Rigorous) (Skill 2.5)

    A. One-to-one reading conferences with students

    B. One-to-one letter sound relationship in spelling

    C. One-to-one reading/pointing of a word to what is on the page

    D. One-to-one matching of students to an appropriate text

Answer: C. One-to-one reading/pointing of a word to what is on the page
When students read, they move from left to right and match each spoken word to a word that appears on the page.

23. **What is the purpose of before reading activities?**
    (Rigorous) (Skill 2.6)

    A. To check if a text is appropriate for a student

    B. To activate background knowledge of readers

    C. To give them a task to complete during reading

    D. To give students a list of vocabulary words to learn

Answer: B. To activate background knowledge of readers
It is necessary to get students thinking about what they are about to read about. This helps to improve comprehension during reading if they are already thinking about the topic presented in the book.

24. **What does "Story Mapping" have children do?**
    (Rigorous) (Skill 2.7)

    A. The students retell the story details

    B. Identify the characters, setting, problem and solution

    C. Identify the main idea and supporting details

    D. Draw a map to show what the characters did

Answer: B. Identify the characters, setting, problem and solution
When students map a story, they identify the characters, setting, problem, and solution. It is best to use this strategy with stories that have only a few characters and have obvious problems and solutions.

25. **What are the two basic types of questions?**
    (Rigorous) (Skill 2.7)

    A.   Easy and hard questions

    B.   Verbal and written questions

    C.   In the book and in the reader's head

    D.   Teacher made and student made

Answer: C. In the book and in the reader's head
Although all choices are two types of questions, in reading there are questions that be answered by looking in the book and questions that can be answered with thinking.

26. **What is the definition of synthesis?**
    (Average) (Skill 2.8)

    A.   Pulling different ideas into one

    B.   Putting a lot of different opinions together

    C.   Taking a whole and pulling it apart

    D.   Oral reading using various voices

Answer: A. Pulling different ideas into one
Synthesis is the opposite of analysis. We take different things and make them one whole thing.

27. **Book reviews are a good source for teaching students about valid and invalid opinions.**
    (Average) (Skill 2.8)

    A.   True

    B.   False

Answer: A. True
Yes. Book reviews are a great source for teaching students about valid and invalid opinions. Opinions in book reviews often contain support for the opinion offered.

28. **In what book would students locate alternative synonyms for words?**
    (Average) (Skill 2.9)

    A. Almanac

    B. Dictionary

    C. Thesaurus

    D. Encyclopedia

Answer: C. Thesaurus
A thesaurus offers alternative synonyms for words to offer a variety of word choices for students. A dictionary gives the definitions of words.

29. **What words should students look for to help direct the next step in a written direction?**
    (Average) (Skill 2.10)

    A. Next

    B. Then

    C. Finally

    D. All of the above

Answer: D. All of the above
Students should look for all of the above words when navigating through written directions.

30. **What are students expected to do when a directive reads, "Support your answer with evidence from the story"?**
    (Rigorous) (Skill 2.10)

    A. Write a one-word response

    B. Recall from memory what they read
    C. Find a few examples in the story and include them in the answer

    D. Name the characters, setting, problem, and solution that are present in the story

Answer: C. Find a few examples in the story and include them in the answer
The best-written responses include a few examples from the story to support what the students believe.

Answer Key: Reading

1. B
2. A
3. C
4. B
5. C
6. C
7. A
8. D
9. A
10. B
11. C
12. A
13. C
14. D
15. B
16. D
17. D
18. B
19. A
20. C
21. C
22. C
23. B
24. B
25. C
26. A
27. A
28. C
29. D
30. C

Rigor Table: Reading

	Easy 20%	Average 40%	Rigorous 40%
Questions	5, 8, 10, 11, 12, 13	1, 9, 14, 15, 17, 18, 19, 20, 26, 27, 28, 29	2, 3, 4, 6, 7, 16, 21, 22, 23, 24, 25, 30

MATH

1. Evaluate:

$$\frac{1}{3} - \frac{1}{2} + \frac{1}{6}$$

   (Average) (Skill 3.1)

   A. 5/6
   B. 2/3
   C. 0
   D. 1

Answer: C. 0

$$\frac{1}{3} - \frac{1}{2} + \frac{1}{6} = \frac{2}{6} - \frac{3}{6} + \frac{1}{6} = \frac{2-3+1}{6} = 0$$

2. Express in symbols: "x is greater than seven and less than or equal to fifteen"?
   (Easy) (Skill 3.3)

   A. $7 < x \leq 15$

   B. $7 > x \geq 15$

   C. $15 \leq x < 7$

   D. $7 < x = 15$

Answer: A. $7 < x \leq 15$

3. "Twice the product of two positive numbers is equal to the square of their sums."
   This statement is:
   (Average) (Skill 3.4)

   A. Always true

   B. Sometimes true

   C. Never true

   D. Meaningless

Answer: C. Never true
Let the two numbers be x and y
Twice their product = 2xy
Square of their sums = $(x+y)^2 = x^2 + 2xy + y^2$
$2xy \neq x^2 + 2xy + y^2$

4. The digit 4 in the number 302.41 is in the
   (Easy) (Skill 3.5)

   A. Tenths place

   B. Ones place

   C. Hundredths place

   D. Hundreds place

Answer: A. Tenths place

5. A carton of milk priced at $6.00 is 30% off. Another carton priced at $5.80 is 20% off. Which one is the better buy?
   (Rigorous) (Skill 3.6)

   A.   The $5.80 carton

   B.   The $6.00 carton

   C.   Both are equal

   D.   There is not enough information

Answer: B. The $6.00 carton
The sale price of the $6.00 carton = $6.00 × 0.7 = $4.20
The sale price of the $5.80 carton = $5.80 × 0.8 = $4.64
Hence, the $6.00 carton is the better buy.

6. **Simplify:**

$$\frac{2^{-4} \times 4^2 \times 8}{4^{-2}}$$

   (Average) (Skill 3.7)

   A. 2^7

   B.   32

   C. $\frac{1}{8}$

   D.   2

Answer: A. 2^7

$$\frac{2^{-4} \times 4^2 \times 8}{4^{-2}} = \frac{2^{-4} \times 2^4 \times 2^3}{2^{-4}} = 2^7$$

7. Simplify:

$$\frac{(-2)^3 + 4^2}{3 - 5^2 + 3 \cdot 6}$$

(Rigorous) (Skill 3.8)

    A.   1/2

    B.   -2

    C.   -3.5

    D.   24

Answer: B. -2

$$\frac{(-2)^3 + 4^2}{3 - 5^2 + 3 \cdot 6} = \frac{-8 + 16}{3 - 25 + 18} = \frac{8}{-4} = -2$$

8. Marvin bought a bag of candy. He gave half of the pieces to his friend Mike and one-third of the pieces to his sister Lisa. He ate half of the remaining pieces and had 15 left. How many pieces of candy were in the bag in the beginning?
(Rigorous) (Skill 3.10)

    A.   120

    B.   90

    C.   30

    D.   180

Answer: D. 180
Let the original number of pieces of candy in the bag be x. Mike got x/2 pieces of candy and Lisa got x/3 pieces. The number of pieces left =

$$x - \frac{x}{2} - \frac{x}{3} = \frac{6x}{6} - \frac{3x}{6} - \frac{2x}{6} = \frac{x}{6}$$

After Marvin ate half the remaining pieces x/12 pieces were left.
Since x/12 = 15, the original number of pieces x = 12 x 15 = 180.

9. **Solve for x:**

   7 + 3x − 6 = 3x + 5 − x

   (Average) (Skill 3.11)

   A.   2.5

   B.   4

   C.   4.5

   D.   27

Answer: B. 4
7 + 3x − 6 = 3x + 5 − x; 7 − 6 = 5 − x; -x = 1 − 5 = -4; x = 4.

10. **What is the next term in the sequence:**

    $\frac{2}{7}, \frac{13}{21}, \frac{20}{21}, \frac{9}{7}, \ldots$

    (Rigorous) (Skill 3.12)

    A. $\frac{29}{21}$

    B. $\frac{17}{21}$

    C. $\frac{11}{7}$

    D. $\frac{34}{21}$

Answer: D. $\frac{34}{21}$

This is an arithmetic sequence where each term is obtained by adding the common difference 7/21 or 1/3 to the preceding term. Thus, the next term in the sequence is 9/7 + 1/3 = 34/21.

11. **About how many seconds is a typical human lifespan? (Assume that the average person lives 75 years).**
    (Average) (Skill 4.2)

    A.   2.5 billion

    B.   2.5 million

    C.   2.5 trillion

    D.   250 million

Answer: A. 2.5 billion

$$75 \text{ years} \times \frac{365 \text{ days}}{1 \text{ year}} \times \frac{24 \text{ hours}}{1 \text{ day}} \times \frac{60 \text{ minutes}}{1 \text{ hour}} \times \frac{60 \text{ seconds}}{1 \text{ minute}} = 2365200000$$

12. Which of the following shapes is a rhombus?

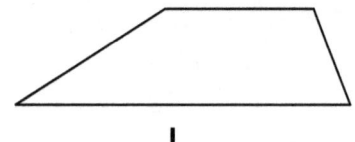

I

II

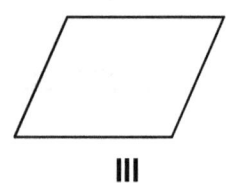

III

(Easy) (Skill 4.3)

A. I

B. II

C. III

D. None of the above

Answer: C. III
A rhombus is a parallelogram with four equal sides.

13. A solid object is shaped like a cone with the top cut off such that the top surface has a radius r_1 and the bottom surface has a radius r_2. If the height of the original cone is h and the height of the part cut off from the top is x, what the volume of the object?

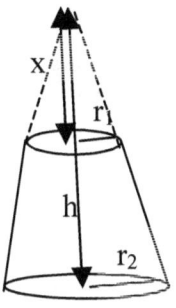

(Rigorous) (Skill 4.4)

A. $\dfrac{1}{3}\pi r_1^2 h - \dfrac{1}{3}\pi r_2^2 x$

B. $\dfrac{1}{3}\pi r_2^2 h + \dfrac{1}{3}\pi r_1^2 x$

C. $\dfrac{1}{3}\pi r_1^2 h + \dfrac{1}{3}\pi r_2^2 x$

D. $\dfrac{1}{3}\pi r_2^2 h - \dfrac{1}{3}\pi r_1^2 x$

Answer: D. $\dfrac{1}{3}\pi r_2^2 h - \dfrac{1}{3}\pi r_1^2 x$

The volume of a cone of radius r and height h is $\dfrac{\pi r^2 h}{3}$. The volume of the object is the volume of the original cone minus the volume of the conical part that is cut off.

14. The slope of the line joining the two points shown on the coordinate plane below is
    (Rigorous) (Skill 4.5)

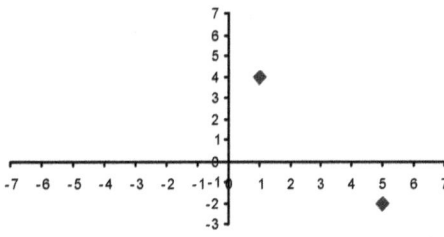

   A.   3/2

   B.   -3/2

   C.   2/3

   D.   -2/3

Answer: B. -3/2
The two points shown are (1,4) and (5,-2). Hence the slope is:
$\dfrac{-2-4}{5-1} = \dfrac{-6}{4} = \dfrac{-3}{2}$.

15. The stem and leaf plot below shows the heights of several children in a class in feet. What is the median height?

3	6 9
4	1 2 3 4 4 9
5	1 3 5

(Average) (Skill 5.1)

   A.   4 ft

   B.   4.9 ft

   C.   4.4 ft

   D.   5.1 ft

Answer: C. 4.4 ft.

16. Which of the following statements is not true about the graph shown below?
(Average) (Skill 5.2)

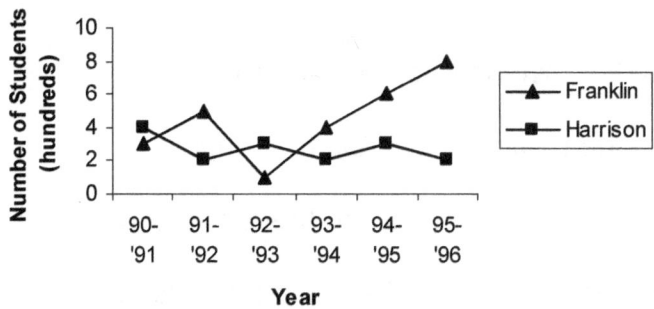

- A. Franklin school shows a rising trend in student enrollment
- B. Harrison school shows a falling trend in student enrollment
- C. Both schools show similar trends in student enrollment
- D. Neither school has had more than 900 students

Answer: C. Both schools show similar trends in student enrollment

17. You wish to create a visual display showing test score trends over several decades for a school. What kind of chart would be the most suitable?
(Average) (Skill 5.3)

- A. Circle graph
- B. Bar graph
- C. Histogram
- D. Line graph

Answer: D. Line graph
A line graph with the years plotted along the horizontal axis would be the best visual display of trends.

18. Which of these statements about the following data set is correct?

    2, 5, 12, 6, 3, 9, 5, 12, 20, 2, 3, 5, 21, 12

    (Rigorous) (Skill 5.4)

    A.   There are 2 modes, the median is 8.5 and the range is 10

    B.   There are 2 modes, the median is 5.5 and the range is 19

    C.   There are 4 modes, the median is 5.5 and the range is 19

    D.   There are 2 modes, the median is 5.5 and the range is 10

Answer: B. There are 2 modes, the median is 5.5 and the range is 19
The two modes are 5 and 12 since they each occur 3 times.

19. A student does the fraction addition $\frac{3}{5} + \frac{4}{15} + \frac{3}{4}$ and gets the answer 5/12. The most likely explanation for this mistake is:
    (Average) (Competency 6)

    A.   The student added all the numerators together and all the denominators together

    B.   The student subtracted the last fraction instead of adding

    C.   The student multiplied the fractions

    D.   None of the above

Answer: A. The student added all the numerators together and all the denominators together
Adding all the numerators together and the denominators together will give 10/24 = 5/12.

20. **A student argues that the tenths place should be the second place to the right of the decimal point since the tens place is the second place to the left of the decimal point. How can you best explain why that is not the case?**
    (Rigorous) (Competency 6)

    A. The decimal point stands for the missing place

    B. There is no "oneths" place since that would be the same as the ones place

    C. Each place, with or without the decimal point is a tenth of the place to its left

    D. There is no "zeroth" place

Answer: C. Each place, with or without the decimal point is a tenth of the place to its left
Answer C would be the most logical answer since you can show that tens is ten times one, one is ten times tenth, and so on. The decimal point merely marks the point between whole numbers and fractions.

21. **You are teaching a group of students how to solve percentage problems. Which of the following concepts would be most helpful to them?**
    (Average) (Competency 6)

    A. To convert a fraction to percent, multiply by 100

    B. "Percent" means "out of 100" and "of" implies multiplication

    C. A percentage problem is essentially a proportion problem with the percentage being the proportion out of 100

    D. To find a given percent of a particular number, divide the number by 100 and multiply by the number given

Answer: C. A percentage problem is essentially a proportion problem with the percentage being the proportion out of 100
While all of the above choices are correct, the concept in choice C is the broadest one that applies to different kinds of percentage problems.

22. **A student performs the computation**

$$(2^3)^5 = 2^8$$

**since exponents are supposed to be added.
How would you explain the error?**
(Easy) (Competency 6)

- A. Say that if a second exponent is outside the parentheses, the two exponents must be multiplied

- B. Note that the following rule must be followed: $(a^m)^n = a^{mn}$

- C. Show that $(2^3)^5 = 8^5$

- D. Show that $(2^3)^5 = 2^3 \times 2^3 \times 2^3 \times 2^3 \times 2^3 = 2^{3+3+3+3+3}$

Answer: D. Show that $(2^3)^5 = 2^3 \times 2^3 \times 2^3 \times 2^3 \times 2^3 = 2^{3+3+3+3+3}$
The choice D clarifies the meaning of exponentiation.

23. **A student uses the mnemonic "PEDMSA" to remember the order of operations. Is she right?**
(Easy) (Competency 6)

- A. Yes

- B. No

- C. It depends on the problem

- D. Switching D and M would be fine but not switching A and S

Answer: A. Yes
Since multiplication and division are equivalent and addition and subtraction are equivalent, PEDMSA is equivalent to PEMDAS.

24. A paraprofessional is helping students learn how to set up and solve systems of equations through the following word problem:

"Three apples and two oranges cost $1.40. Four apples and three oranges cost $2.00. How much does one apple and one orange cost?"

Which of the following steps would you use:

I. Use the guess and check method to estimate the answer.
II. Identify and name the variables.
III. Write equations showing the relationships between the variables.
IV. Subtract the cost of three apples and two oranges from the cost of four apples and three oranges.
V. Solve the equations using substitution or elimination.

(Rigorous) (Competency 6)

A. I, II, III, and V

B. II, III, and V

C. I and IV

D. IV

Answer: B. II, III, and V
Although I and IV are valid ways to approach and solve this particular problem, the goal of this lesson is learning to set up and solve a system of equations. Only steps II, III, and V are related to this objective.

25. **A student is solving the equation**

    x + 3 = 2(x + 3)

    He divides both sides by x + 3 and gets 1 = 2. What is his mistake?
    (Rigorous) (Competency 6)

    A. He did not make any mistakes

    B. He inadvertently divided by zero

    C. One can never divide by an algebraic expression

    D. He should have first set x + 3 = y

Answer: B. He inadvertently divided by zero
Distributing the right side, we see that x + 3 = 2x + 6; or x = -3. Hence x + 3 = 0 and dividing by x + 3 is essentially dividing by zero..

26. **You are helping a student find the next term in a given number sequence. A good first step would be to**
    (Easy) (Competency 6)

    A. Check and see whether the sequence is arithmetic or geometric

    B. Take the difference of the first two terms and add it to the last term

    C. Take the ratio of the first two terms and multiply the last term by it

    D. Check to see whether alternate terms are related

Answer is A. Check and see whether the sequence is arithmetic or geometric
Arithmetic and geometric sequences are the most common type of number sequences.

27. A paraprofessional is giving real life examples in order to explain the relative magnitude of the length units millimeter, centimeter, and meter. Which of the following sets would be the best choice?
(Average) (Competency 6)

   A.   Items on sale at a store

   B.   Animals of different sizes

   C.   Objects in a classroom

   D.   Toys of various sizes

Answer: C. Objects in a classroom
Objects available at hand are the best choice since the students can hold and measure them.

28. Students in a class are asked to draw the parallelogram with the largest possible area with longer sides 4 cm in length and shorter sides 2 cm in length. Student A draws a parallelogram with an internal angle of 90 degrees. Student B, C, and D draw parallelograms with internal angles of 45 degrees, 120 degrees, and 60 degrees respectively. Which student has the correct answer?
(Rigorous) (Competency 6)

   A.   A

   B.   B

   C.   C

   D.   D

Answer: A. A
The area of a parallelogram is the product of its base and height. It clear from the drawings below that parallelograms with the same dimensions will get smaller in area as the acute angles get smaller. Hence the parallelogram with the largest area is the rectangle with an internal angle of 90 degrees.

29. A student is computing the area of a right triangle on a coordinate plane defined by the points A (-1, 0), B (0, 2) and C (6, -1). Which of the following is the simplest method?
(*Rigorous*) *(Competency 6)*

   A. Draw a perpendicular BD from B to AC and find the coordinates of D using the Pythagorean theorem on triangles ABD and DBC; find the height BD of the triangle; area = ½ x AC x BD

   B. The coordinate axes cut the triangle into four shapes; find the area of each shape and add them up

   C. Identify the two perpendicular sides using slopes and find their lengths; if one of the sides is the base, the other is the height; area = ½ x base x height

   D. Find the equation of the line BC; find the point D at which the line BC intersects the y axis; find the areas of the triangles BAD and CBD and add them

Answer: C. Identify the two perpendicular sides using slopes and find their lengths; if one of the sides is the base, the other is the height; area = ½ x base x height
Method C takes only three simple steps. The other methods will work but will take many more complicated steps.

30. You are helping a student graph yearly rainfall data in inches for a century. A good choice of scale for the x and y axes would be
    (Average) (Competency 6)

    A. Years along the x-axis with major tick marks every decade and inches along the y-axis with major tick marks every 5 inches

    B. Years along the y-axis with major tick marks every decade and inches along the x-axis with major tick marks every 5 inches

    C. Years along the x-axis with major tick marks every year and inches along the y-axis with major tick marks every 5 inches

    D. Years along the x-axis with major tick marks every decade and inches along the y-axis with major tick marks every inch

Answer: A. Years along the x-axis with major tick marks every decade and inches along the y-axis with major tick marks every 5 inches
Year is the independent variable here and should be plotted along the x axis. The major tick marks should be chosen so that there are not more than 10–15 on each axis.

Answer Key: Mathematics

1.	C		16.	C
2.	A		17.	D
3.	C		18.	B
4.	A		19.	A
5.	B		20.	C
6.	A		21.	C
7.	B		22.	D
8.	D		23.	A
9.	B		24.	B
10.	D		25.	B
11.	A		26.	A
12.	C		27.	C
13.	D		28.	A
14.	B		29.	C
15.	C		30.	A

Rigor Table: Mathematics

	Easy 20%	Average 40%	Rigorous 40%
Question	2, 4, 12, 22, 23, 26	1, 3, 6, 9, 11, 15, 16, 17, 19, 21, 27, 30	5, 7, 8, 10, 13, 14, 18, 20, 24, 25, 28, 29

WRITING

1. **What type of writing includes headings, subheadings, and titles?** *(Average) (Skill 1.7)*

    A. Persuasive

    B. Descriptive

    C. Narrative

    D. Informative

Answer: D. Informative
Informative writing is usually non-fiction, and non-fiction writing normally has headings, subheadings, and titles.

2. **Which word needs to be corrected in the sentence below?** *(Rigorous) (Skill 1.8)*

    The Biggilow family were concerned with the appearance of their home.

    A. family

    B. were

    C. appearance

    D. their

Answer: B. were
The Biggilow family is considered a singular. Therefore, the correct word is *was*.

3. Which word will complete the sentence?
   (Average) (Skill 1.8)

   It will be ____ cold for us to camp outside this weekend.

   A. too

   B. to

   C. two

   D. tow

Answer: A. too
Too shows extremes or means "also." In this sentence, the weather will be below an acceptable temperature so camping will not be an option.

4. Which sentence is punctuated incorrectly?
   (Easy) (Skill 1.8)

   A. Tomorrow night we'll have pizza for dinner?

   B. Close the door please.

   C. Go away!

   D. What time does the movie begin?

Answer: A. Tomorrow night we'll have pizza for dinner?
Alone, this is a statement and should be punctuated with a period – not a question mark.

5. Which punctuation mark is required, if any, in the sentence?
    (Skill 1.8, Easy)

    Let's have some chocolate graham crackers and marshmallows for dessert

    A. !

    B. ?

    C. ,

    D. None

Answer: C. ,
A comma placed between chocolate and graham crackers now suggests that three items are needed for dessert rather than two (chocolate graham crackers and marshmallows).

6. What type of sentence is the sentence below?
    (Rigorous) (Skill 1.8)

    Millie and Max seemed tired and bored.

    A. Simple

    B. Compound

    C. Complex

    D. Compound/complex

Answer: A. Simple
The sentence has a compound subject but there is only one verb. Therefore, it is a simple sentence.

7. **How would a letter to the editor be written?**
   (Rigorous) (Skill 1.10)

   A. Using formal language

   B. Using informal/slang language

   C. Using informal language with informal mechanics

   D. Using words from the dialect of its intended audience

Answer: A. Using formal language
Normally, a letter to the editor is written to persuade others to think in one way or defend a position. Therefore, it is most likely going to be written using formal language.

8. **How do you write the plural form of the word *tornado*?**
   (Easy) (Skill 7.1)

   A. Tornados

   B. Tornadoes

   C. Tornadose

   D. Tornadoz

Answer: B. Tornadoes
Words like *tornado, buffalo,* and *tomato* have an *–es* added to them for the plural form.

9. **Which word best completes the sentence?**
   (Easy) (Skill 7.1)

   There were two _____ swimming in the fish bowl.

   A.   fishes

   B.   fish

   C.   fishies

   D.   fish's

Answer: B. fish
Fish is *fish* when it is both singular and plural.

10. **Which word will complete the sentence?**
    (Average) (Skill 7.2)

    We are so happy that _____ joining us on our annual vacation to the mountains.

    A.   they're

    B.   their

    C.   there

    D.   them

Answer: A. they're
They're is a contraction for "they are". If *they are* is substituted, "We are happy that they are joining us on our vacation to the mountains," it still makes sense. Therefore, it is evident which form of the word to use.

11. Carrie pointed to a house on Pritchett Drive and said, "I used to live there"
    Was Carrie's statement said correctly?
    (Easy) (Skill 7.2)

    A.   Yes

    B.   No

Answer: A. Yes
Use to is often substituted for *used to*. Carried pronounced this correctly.

12. Which word will complete the sentence?
    (Rigorous) (Skill 7.3)

    The _____ live in a rocky area at the zoo.

    A.   monkeys

    B.   monkey's

    C.   monkies

    D.   monkie's

Answer: A. monkeys
The correct spelling of the plural form of *monkey* is *monkeys*.

13. Which sentence is correct?
    (Rigorous) (Skill 7.3)

    A.   Kids running around on a beautiful spring day.

    B.   Kids run around on a beautiful spring day.

    C.   Kids run, around on a beautiful spring day.

    D.   Kids running. Around on a beautiful spring day.

Answer: B. Kids run around on a beautiful spring day.
When the verb *running* is used it creates a phrase or dependent clause rather than a sentence. Therefore, B is the correct answer because the verb *run* is used to create a complete sentence.

14. **What type of sentence is the sentence below?**
    (Average) (Skill 7.4)

    While swimming in the pool, the children had a great time together.

    A. Simple

    B. Compound

    C. Complex

    D. Compound/Complex

Answer C. Complex
This sentence consists of an independent clause (the children had a great time together) plus a dependent clause (While swimming in the pool).

15. **What must be done to make this sentence correct?**
    (Rigorous) (Skill 7.4)

    Meanwhile in the living room.

    A. Place a comma after meanwhile

    B. Change the word *living room* to *livingroom*

    C. Delete the period and add an independent clause

    D. Choice A and C

Answer: D. Choice A and C
Meanwhile is a transition word that needs to be followed by a comma. In order for the sentence to be complete, an independent clause must be added.

16. **Which sentence is a run-on sentence?**
    (Rigorous) (Skill 7.4)

    A. I would like to have a grilled chicken salad for lunch what would you like.

    B. For lunch I had grilled chicken a diet soda and a bag of chips.

    C. Before lunch I washed my hands then I bought a soda.

    D. As soon as I finished my lunch I returned to my office to finish my work.

Answer: A, This choice contains a statement and a question in one sentence.
This is the run-on and must have a period between the statement and the question asked.

17. **Which change, if any, would make the underlined words correct?**
    (Easy) (Skill 7.5)

    <u>Them</u> put their feet in the water while they <u>was</u> sitting on the dock.

    A. They...was

    B. Them...were

    C. They...were

    D. No change necessary

Answer: C. They...were
They and *were* are the correct words. *Were* is the correct past tense form that must be used in this sentence.

18. **Which change, if any, would make the underlined word correct?**
    (Rigorous) (Skill 7.5)

    I can't believe that you brang that topic up at the staff meeting yesterday.

    A. bring

    B. brought

    C. brung

    D. No change necessary

Answer: B. brought
The correct past tense of the word "to bring" is *brought*.

19. **Which word will make the sentence correct?**
    (Easy) (Skill 7.5)

    In the _____ the housing market was booming and people's profit margins were a lot larger.

    A. 1990's

    B. 1990s

    C. nineteen-nineties

    D. 19-nineties

Answer: B. 1990s
The plurals of letters, numbers, and abbreviations are made by adding *s*.

20. **Which sentence is written correctly?**
    (Easy) (Skill 7.5)

    A. I gathered all the garbage together and thowed it all away.

    B. I gathered all the garbage together and through it all away.

    C. I gathered all the garbage together and threw it all away.

    D. I gathered all the garbage together and thrown it all away.

Answer: C. I gathered all the garbage together and threw it all away.
The correct past tense form of the verb *to throw* is *threw*.

21. **Which word will correctly complete the sentence?**
    (Average) (Skill 7.5)

    We waited in the _____ office for over an hour for our appointment.

    A. doctores

    B. doctors

    C. doctors'

    D. doctor

Answer: C. doctors'
The word *doctors'* indicates that the office belongs to more than one doctor.

Directions: Choose the correctly spelled word to complete each sentence for questions 22–26

22. **For spring vacation, our family decided to visit a _____ island.**
    (Average) (Skill 7.6)

    A.   tropickal

    B.   tropical

Answer: B. tropical
The letter *c* makes the *k* sound in this word.

23. **The sign at the intersection told us to _____ with caution.**
    (Average) (Skill 7.6)

    A.   proceed

    B.   preceed

Answer: A. proceed
Preceed means "to come before." *Proceed* means to go, or move ahead.

24. **Queen Elizabeth became _____ when she tripped and fell down the winding, circular staircase.**
    (Average) (Skill 7.6)

    A.   embarrassed

    B.   embarrassed

Answer A. embarrassed
There are two r's and two s's.

25. **She serves as a _____ for human resources and corporate headquarters.**
    (Average) (Skill 7.6)

    A.   liaison
    B.   liason

Answer: B. liason
Although the second *i* isn't often heard, *liaison* has and *i* surrounding the *a*.

26. **The bag says that this recipe will _____ 6-dozen cookies.**
    (Average) (Skill 7.6)

    A. yield
    B. yeild

Answer: A. yield
Even though the vowel team of *ie* usually makes the /i/ sound, when /ie/ are together the *e* sound is heard instead.

27. **When a student is going to write a non-fiction essay, what is the best way to organize their ideas?**
    (Rigorous) (Skill 8.1)

    A. Create an outline

    B. Create a web

    C. Free write ideas on a topic

    D. All of the above

Answer: D. All of the above
Prewriting is the stage that organizes and gets student's ideas in one place.

28. **What is the purpose of prewriting before students draft?**
    (Average) (Skill 8.1)

    A. It helps organize their ideas

    B. If they prewrite, they don't need to draft

    C. It will make their draft longer

    D. A prewrite and a draft are the same thing

Answer: A. It helps organize their ideas
Prewrites help to organize student ideas so that when they draft their topic will be narrow and manageable.

29. **What makes the organizer, or prewrite, for a personal narrative unique?**
    (Rigorous) (Skill 8.1)

    A. It includes characters, setting, problem, and a solution

    B. It includes a beginning, middle, and end

    C. It outlines how the piece will be organized; for example, a circle story

    D. It lists out the sequence of events with headings

Answer: A. It includes characters, setting, problem, and a solution
Although all of the choices above will go into planning a personal narrative, students must decide who the characters will be, where the story will take place, what the problem is, and how the problem will be solved. Without these ideas established, it is too likely that the piece will not be focused and the author will likely get off track in their writing.

30. **A student is trying to find synonyms for the word *nice*. What is the best reference source use?**
    (Rigorous) (Skill 8.2)

    A. A dictionary

    B. An atlas

    C. An almanac

    D. A thesaurus

Answer: D. A thesaurus
A thesaurus is a great tool that lists synonyms and antonyms for words.

31. **Look at the dictionary entry below.**

    chocolate [chaw-kuh-lit]
    1. a preparation of the seeds of cacao, roasted, husked, and ground, often sweetened and flavored, as with vanilla.

    How many syllables does the word chocolate have according to the dictionary entry?
    (Rigorous) (Skill 8.2)

    A. 1

    B. 2

    C. 3

    D. 4

Answer: C. 3
Even though chocolate sounds like it may have 2 syllables, in fact, it has 3 [chaw-kuh-lit].

32. **What is a revising strategy that students can use to improve their drafts?**
    (Rigorous) (Skill 8.3)

    A. Try different types of beginnings

    B. Read the piece backwards to focus on the spelling of each word

    C. Make sure that each sentence begins with a capital letter

    D. Make sure that each sentence has end punctuation

Answer: A. Try different types of beginnings
Papers can begin with a variety of different beginnings and good writers try a variety of beginnings to improve reader interest.

33. **What is the purpose of a thesis statement?**
    (Average) (Skill 8.3)

    A. To keep the writer focused

    B. To state the main idea of a paper

    C. To give the writer something to research

    D. To act as a hook

Answer: B. To state the main idea of a paper
The thesis statement's purpose is to let the reader know what the essay will be about. In other words, it is the main idea of the paper.

34. **In a five-paragraph essay, what are the middle paragraphs called?**
    (Average) (Skill 8.3)

    A. Thesis statement

    B. The introduction

    C. The body

    D. The conclusion

Answer: C. The body
The body is the largest, most informative part of a five-paragraph essay.

35. **What is the first sentence in every body paragraph called?**
    (Average) (Skill 8.3)

    A. The main idea

    B. The thesis statement

    C. Opinion support statement

    D. The question statement

Answer: A. The main idea
Each topic sentence of each body paragraph reflects the central idea of the paragraph it introduces. In other words, it states the main idea of the body paragraph it introduces.

36. **Why must students edit their papers before they publish them?** *(Average) (Skill 8.4)*

    A.   To find pictures to use before the piece is published

    B.   Because papers must be done in a student's neatest handwriting

    C.   To improve the craft of writing

    D.   To improve spelling, punctuation, and grammar

Answer: D. To improve spelling, punctuation, and grammar
Editing is the last step in writing before the piece is ready to be published. This is where the writer checks the spelling, punctuation, and grammar usage.

37. **What is the best way to edit a paper if it has been handwritten?** *(Rigorous) (Skill 8.4)*

    A.   Scan it and spell check it

    B.   Have the teacher review it

    C.   Read it backwards and have a peer review it

    D.   Have an adult review the paper and make corrections

Answer: C. Read it backwards and have a peer review it
Peer editing has many advantages. It gets students involved in the editing process and allows students to use upper level thinking skills.

38. How do authors determine whether their piece should be formal or informal?
(Average) (Skill 8.5)

    A.   Whether they will be graded by the teacher

    B.   If the writer is trying to entertain, inform, or persuade

    C.   By the language that was used in the piece of writing

    D.   Whether the writing is formal or informal

Answer: B. If the writer is trying to entertain, inform, or persuade
Each piece of writing has one of three purposes: to entertain, to inform, or to persuade. The purpose of the piece will drive what type of language will be used.

39. What is a persuasive technique that simply states the same idea many times only using different words each time to convey the same idea?
(Rigorous) (Skill 8.6)

    A.   Fallacious reasoning

    B.   Only-cause fallacy

    C.   Circular reasoning

    D.   A hasty generalization

Answer: C. Circular reasoning
Circular reasoning is an illogical attempt at persuasion. However, the argument simply goes in circles and does not offer any logical support.

40. *There are a few holidays that recognize saints. For example, Valentine's Day recognizes Saint Valentine. St. Patrick's Day recognizes St. Patrick.*

What type of writing is demonstrated in the passage above? (Rigorous) (Skill 8.6)

    A.   Descriptive

    B.   Narrative

    C.   Informative

    D.   Persuasive

Answer: C. Informative
The passage was written to inform the reader about certain holidays that we celebrate as recognition of certain saints.

Answer Key: Writing

1.	D	21.	C
2.	B	22.	B
3.	A	23.	A
4.	A	24.	A
5.	C	25.	B
6.	A	26.	A
7.	A	27.	D
8.	B	28.	A
9.	B	29.	A
10.	A	30.	D
11.	A	31.	C
12.	A	32.	A
13.	B	33.	B
14.	C	34.	C
15.	D	35.	A
16.	A	36.	D
17.	C	37.	C
18.	B	38.	B
19.	B	39.	C
20.	C	40.	C

Rigor Table: Writing

	Easy 20%	Average 40%	Rigorous 40%
Questions	4, 5, 8, 9, 11, 17, 19, 20	1, 3, 10, 14, 21, 22, 23, 24, 25, 26, 28, 33, 34, 35, 36, 38	2, 6, 7, 12, 13, 15, 16, 18, 27, 29, 30, 31, 32, 37, 39, 40